When the Time Comes

Helen Swain

When the Time Comes

When the Time Comes
ISBN 978 1 76109 448 4
Copyright © text Helen Swain 2022
Cover image: Diana Mills

First published 2022 by
Ginninderra Press
PO Box 3461 Port Adelaide 5015
www.ginninderrapress.com.au

Contents

Family	9
My father	10
My mother	11
Me	12
Visiting	13
Shine your shoes	16
Back to the present	18
Reality	19
I will ring	20
There is a place	21
Respite	22
Adapting	23
No worries	24
Colliding worlds	25
Out and about	26
Every night	27
Trial and error	28
Scrabbling through the days	29
Holes in my dreams	30
I wish to know more	31
The tree of knowledge	32
This I know	33
Flickering	34
The doctor	35
Routines	36
Second package	38
Third package	40
Fourth package	41
What do you know	42
Lapsed	43

Sharing the times	44
The future	45
Still the father says	46
Mum's war	47
Loose dreams	48
Missing	49
Home comforts	57
Hectoring	58
Resentment	59
What do you do?	60
Searching for positivity	62
Home help day	63
A matter of course	64
Sunday evening is full of grace	67
Slow drops of time	69
Another year: another Monday	70
Attempting a treaty	71
A small offering	72
It's not a dream	74
Lullaby	76
2 a.m.	77
When the time comes	78
Redeemed by the mind's eye	80
B flat in 3 minor parts	81
Multiplicity	82
Communion	83
Mum's teeth	84
Check	85
When help is needed	86
Call the doctor service	88
All I want	90
How to measure time	91

Getting a grip	92
I am no longer alone	93
The small hours	94
Belonging	95
A piece of business	96
Biding	97
At your funeral	98
Today's lesson	99
Acknowledgements	100

Dedicated to all the unseen, unheard
and uncomplaining carers of those in need.

Family

Like possums
we are a small private family
not prone to sing
or invite others in.
We keep our distance
from you
and from each other.

My father

He didn't ask me.
He said, between breaths
and that made a difference
the between breaths
you
look after
your Mum
Clare.

He didn't say Clare
but it's what he meant
he meant me.

Knowing this conversation
is likely the last
you listen with everything
attend as if these words
are holy
a message
from the other side.

My mother

When Dad got sick
Mum had a sudden thought

I don't want to be a burden
she told me
when the time comes
just put me out of my misery

This request
for either more love
or less life
came with no instructions.

At the time
I was not worried
by words without substance.

Me

At the moment I am between dogs
but after 53 years of working life
I am ready to set up my own kennels

with a 'Dogs First' slogan.
I think of how aggressive dogs
respond to massage, love, stability.

I fan my intentions each night
me, my real self, making a difference.
I'll start with used greyhounds.

If Mum needs looking after
she can go into a home.
I'd be no good at it, I couldn't do it.

I am not thinking of looking after my mother
I say again this is what I refuse to consider.
I volunteer at the local dog's home

keep an eye out for a suitable fit.
I apply to do ballroom dancing.

In the travel agent on Collins Street
I ask about Darwin as a stepping-off point.

Visiting

1.

I open the door
call
Mum

Once the front hall
was a hall

now, a passageway
to be negotiated.

Chairs fully flummoxed
droop beside wanton tables.

Under boxes, bags suffocate
their contents.

The untold
flows down the walls.

I call
Mum

and know already
what lies in store.

2.

Here in my mother's house
her hands flap determined to control

the words coming out of her mouth
cheesing she says and stops.

We don't understand
question whether it matters.

I put the rabbit out for Robert
she says at last.

She flaunts her memory loss
tosses our past into the compost.

She is so careless of photos
we used to call family stories.

3.

In the fridge
it could have been cabbage, limp purple
and dark blue cream set beside
the carefully wrapped dish mop
butter scum, splintered cheese.

Something slips from my mind.
Who is this person?
Who owns this fridge?

I think of dog comfort
the heft of breath.

Shine your shoes

has become a mantra
melding past and present
rising from when a man
came to our place before teatime
go outside and play.
Pup and I couldn't hear but
when he dissolved into the twilight
there was talking in the kitchen
as if the man had brought a key
to unlock our silence.
I was told that Mum would work
at O'Reilly's Shoes!

In the clear cold mornings
my mother walked down the hill
to the shop and was encased
in a high glass office.
Here she waited for a bell
to ring on the counter below
signalling money in a tin
would sail across the ceiling
for her to take out
and find change that slid on the thin string
back to the counter.

Standing at the shop window after school,
I watched this queenly mother
receive the vanishing money
when Eileen Harris and Christine Quinn
bought new school shoes.
Watching their feet under the desk the next day
I was a princess, secretly laced to my mother
through the shine and smell of new leather.
Shine your shoes, shine your shoes
is still her shuffling motto.

Back to the present

Oh Dad, what did you expect
when you said *Look after…*?
Mum needs to go into a home.

Don't worry, she won't hear me.
Yesterday she planted her hearing aid
in a bowl of milk in the fridge

which is all right for you, you're dead.

What happens	
when	
there are holes	in your head?
Mr Mrs	blank
a thought	
used to be	words
used to be.	

My tongue presses a sourness
against the roof of my mouth.
I try to remember tender.

I could stay with her
for the time being.

Reality

Our doctor says to think about it.
You should think about a home you know
at least get her name down.
It's hard to put a time frame
round these things
but looking after her won't be easy.

Another urine infection now
but swooping towards mindless mutter
where the reasonable
is confused and some improbable
state of personal hygiene
becomes a thing of the past

on into the middle stage.
At night, seeing me as intruder
unmerciful tramp.

I will ring

It is not a failure
they tell me
but a healthy choice.

Heather from the dog's home
her mum's in one
down in Glenorchy

she says it's ok
she's just lonely
that's all.

There is a place

an answer
from a home
only three suburbs away.

This facility will take her
for two weeks.

It's called respite, this short stay
and we can see.

There is a waiting list
for permanency

but for two weeks we'll see
give it a go.

Respite

She's in the Grace Lees Home.
It's for the best.

They aim to make a real difference
by putting people first

getting to know everyone
as individuals

tailoring the care to suit
everyone's needs

especially those facing
end-of-life issues.

They develop meaningful
trusting relationships

people know their loved ones
will be safe and cared for.

I drink sherry
sleep in front of the television

tomorrow I'll organise
something.

Adapting

I watch her walking
up and down the corridors.
I think I know what she's doing
she's looking for the key
hanging on the faded red cord

that lives on the inside of her back door.
I've seen her take it down
from the hook
and carry it off.
Later
when she sees the key in her hand
she goes straight back to the door
and hangs it up.

These are her at home habits
smiling with satisfaction
when she replaces it
but now
in this strange place
she looks anxious.

No worries

I haven't seen her for three days

for three days I have been ringing
to see how it is for her.

For three days they tell me
she seems a little agitated
but is fine, she's doing fine.

And so am I.
I am doing fine.
On Saturday, I took the Dogs' Home dogs to the beach.
On Sunday, I took them to the beach.
On Monday I took them to the beach.

The questions that rise in waves
cannot be answered

there is the question of responsibility
there is the question of alternatives
there is the question of if
and if not
the question of when
and how long will…

Colliding worlds

I learn she is a nuisance
going into anyone's room
and looking behind the door.

She is not allowed
the nurses tell her
in clear firm voices.

She briefly thinks they are mad
and she starts rubbing her hands.
I wonder would it give

her respite
from these irrelevant walls
if I bring her that key.

I notice she and I use
the same body movements.
When I conclude a thought

I like to give my hands
a brief rub.
This action, being so akin to hers

makes me nervous
if I notice myself doing it
and I immediately pat my hair.

When I leave the aged care home
I notice how I rub my hands and pat my hair
as soon as I get out the door.

Out and about

The street fills my disquiet
with movement and I walk
into the Twist Knit Shop
lace knitting classes $170

patterns of a mother
in a rocking chair knitting
complexities of faith
skeins of devotion

I breathe the cleanliness
the washed, carded
spun and dyed certainty
the loosely wound softness

like the careful washing
of a baby's shawl
like the belly
of a freshly killed rabbit.

I remember holding up my hands
while my mother
wound feather-soft skeins into balls
later teaching me 'cat's cradle'.

Every night

They tell me
she takes the plastic liners
out of the bins
shoves her clothes in
sits on the edge
of the bed
cradling her shoes
waiting to go home.

Trial and error

My mother
is not what they are looking for

putting dirty pads
down the loo
hiding them
stuffing paper towelling on top
soiled clothes
at the back of a drawer
where no one checks.

My belly is twisted
caught between desire and duty.

We go home
together.

Scrabbling through the days

She opens the drawer
redeems three unmatched knitting needles

rummages for a futile torch bulb.
I open the cupboard

discover banana we think
we think it was a banana

while she ferrets out
a hundred plastic bread clasps.

We hear them sometimes
scratching at the night.

I burrow in, find a ragged dog collar
sticking to a melted candle.

Coaster and brass lipstick
fight for precedence.

She wants to eat
a small box with hard angry liquorice.

Under the sink, $760
rests in a repellent bucket.

We both forage
see Baby Jesus nestled in a corner

arms outstretched
huffing with irritation.

Holes in my dreams

Half the night and all the day I listen
to Jim Tanner's Doberman

howling discontent as dogs do
barking their faithful mission.

It doesn't get enough walking.
I consider how to kidnap it

set up my own place
for dogs not cared for

owners too old
to look after them

ones that need me
don't you reckon, Dad?

You look after your Mum, Clare.

I will. I'll see to her.

I wish to know more

I wash her hair
feel the hardness of her brow
towel the outside
of her matchstick head
put my lips on her incurious bones.

As a child I do not imagine
a mother going back
before I was born
but now I want
to clothe and furnish
that early one
that led to her becoming
and my becoming.

If she forgets stuff that I don't know
who is she?
Who am I?
Why was I born?

The tree of knowledge

I was shocked to learn
my clean mother
disgraced her family
by falling
pregnant the way walnuts

or bad apples
fall from a tree.
Her own mother staring
straight ahead, refusing to look
or let her come home.

One thing I know
is that she paid for the pram
my whole layette
everything
by shooting rabbits

skinning them
but she never
talks about it.
I'm trying to get hold of mist.
Can you help with that doctor?

I am looking for a state
as yet uncharted
but now, in the kitchen
a breath of abandonment
tenderises me.

This I know

1943/44
She was in the women's land army

up near Brisbane.

She loved it
away from the family farm

this time milking with other girls
and her so efficient

having been brought up to it.

1945
Unmarried

pregnant

me, her gift to the country

a two-ton
shame.

Flickering

She has started saying

We'll have a lamb stew for your father

every day, she sets the table for him

he's dead, Mum   he's died

she realises over and over
like it was the first time.

The doctor

gives us an *End-of-Life Care Directive.*

A death wish-list
with a capacity toolkit
to help us think.

Decision-making
is based on determining
the appropriate phase of care
according to realistic assessment
of the probable outcomes
of medical treatment
at any particular stage

She explains
that we are eligible
for assessment
for assistance.

So that's good.

Routines

We are now
part of a system
there is a service

a package that comes
for two hours
three days a week.

The first one, Emilia
could have stood on one leg
on top of an iced cake

or in a music box
blonde, gorgeous
accent from somewhere.

Mum bit her.
Emilia was reaching over
to comb Mum's hair.

Mum leant forward
and bit her on the soft part
inside upper arm.

Couldn't resist
sinking her teeth in.
There was blood.

Emilia yelled, yanked her arm away
but Mum wouldn't let go.
Emilia hit her.

Mum's teeth were pretty new
only about a year old
so that might have been

part of the problem.
I don't think she meant it
but you can't tell with Mum.

Second package

She was a big woman, Karen.
Without meaning to be rude
she was a bit fat

couldn't move very quickly
and when Mum bailed her up
she couldn't get away.

Mum was pulling at her, pinching
you give them back
they're Raymond's

give me those shoes
you give me those shoes!
Poor Karen

stuck in the corner
with her hands
trying to protect her face

trying to push Mum off.
Karen's big but Mum
a little Rottweiler terrier cross.

I joined in and Mum
collapsed against me crying
she's stolen Raymond's shoes!

Who on earth is Raymond?
Karen is beside herself.
Your mother's not

socialised, she's not fit.
Another helper
hits the dust.

Third package

Bernita was all we ever wished for
we adored her

the way she cleaned poo
off the wall

and stayed cheerful
while she sang 'Forevermore'

until she too was gone
to look after her own mother, apparently.

Fourth package

Wendy comes now.
She's very efficient

and I know
this little package of time

is mine.
I can get my hair cut.

What do you know

about the person you can no longer name?
My mother has stopped calling me Clare.
She still sometimes says dear
but she says dear to most people.

Am I most people?
Are her people interchangeable?
I am surprised by this lack of identifying
how it makes me lose my way.

Lapsed

There was a time
when the midwinter sun called
and my mother would answer.

I can see her strong legs
keeping pace with the wind
as the sea stung and whipped at her skin.

Now I cradle her thin bones as she watches
the green translucent water
catching the low rays of light.

Can she see how it spills diamonds
onto the hungry sand
strand after strand carelessly slipping

from a bolt of perpetual taffeta?
Does her mind still dance
to the hush-hush wishing of waves

while the salt-eaten black rock
uses its sharp edges
to trim her memory?

Sharing the times

When I burnt the casserole
and opened the back door
to get rid of the smoke

a gale blew in
and loosened
all the cobwebs.

Years-old homes
festooned from the ceiling
like inverted parachutes of dust

giving the spiders
and me
a fresh start.

The spiders
immediately
got to work, DIY-style.

Delicate architecture
reassembled
step by step as I watched

vacuum cleaner in hand
prepared and unprepared
to suck up life.

The future

I've found an online course

on how to become a certified
rehabilitation practitioner in
alternative canine techniques.

I could do that
it would help me transition.

Still the father says

You look aft…
I will…
Don't you bear no grudges, Clare-bear

I won't! I say,
but I think,
what the hell would he know?

He was the one Mum always looked after
with his trembling
his night sweats
and silent screams
on and on
back to the Burma railway.
All those bones.

Mum's war

This is what you did isn't it, Mum?
Looked after Dad and
you looked after Pop when
Nanna died and

Nanna seeing to her mum.
You girls all taking it in turns
to sleep with her
which you loved
when you were little
and she made up stories
about the funny animals
staring out from
the knots in the wood

but you hated it
when she got old and
went queer and
pinched you and
she smelt and
you at twelve
expected to share a bed
with your grandmother.

And her mother
did she look after her mother too?
How far back does it go
this snail trail of old skin?

Loose dreams

Here in my chair the afternoon sun
permeates my body like a symphony.
I find it hard to move, in every way prefer
to sit here, watch an ant flow across my skin
minuscule legs weaving its life's pattern
against the back of my hand.

Its tiny black body does not belong in here.
This is our place, dedicated to human content
a citadel built to withstand the intrusion
of ants, but like my mother, it is searching
this domain, as if I have something to offer
something to take home.

Ant, Mum, me; we all wish for an oracle
hoping comprehension will plonk itself down
close by, divulging our intent.
Look how the earth trembles
at the march of the ants.

In the south of Japan
ants have upended a whole island
from within and on the surface.
The sun shines, my eyes close.
I try to imagine.

Missing

1

Mum!
Where is she?
Was that the gate?

A flash of dread bursts through each vein

she hasn't got her stick

wreckage is uppermost

Mum!

Mind's eye
Where?
What?
When?

Mum!

2

I hurry
towards the shops
she could be anywhere
Have you seen?

Graeme Recline's
Second-hand Furniture
she likes that room with no windows
no chance of having to smile

She's wearing, oh what is she wearing?

Try the Seoul Korean BBQ
where we met that artist
who painted people with purple lips
scraped the paint across each face

Mum?

with a pallet knife so all you could see
were the lips no eyes

My mother yes somewhere

stripes of red and yellow.

3

I have options
Maybe call the police
try the newsagency

I stand beside the sign
where I can buy pig's ears
and duck's tongues

I don't know how to cook tongues

immobilised
I think of a megaphone.

4

There she is!
Of course, in the park!

Oh phew! Be still my biting heart.
Oh phew! Be still my beating brain

not mashed up
not mown down
no road, river, rampage, riot

just warm cement
grass, smelling
like lonely nights in summer.

The future dissolves
and here we are
you and I

lives floated together
bumping as barges do
abreast

and apart
thud and scrape
to the tuneless cry

of the ravens
two, in the branch overhead
watching you.

One glides to the ground
black gloss caught in the sun
it bounces its judicial weight

while in the tree
its mate calls a harsh note
descending.

5

What are you calling, Mum?
See the ravens listen
consider your request

and I want to join you
want to stand here
make my voice thin and cracked
call

to no one

if we stay here long enough
someone will come
help us both

what I'm calling
doesn't matter

Caark, caa-ark. Caark caark
Caaaaaaaaaaaaaaaaaaaaaaaaaaaaaaark   Cak.

6

If we were animals
we could stay here forever

you'd be a llama
are they the ones that spit

creep up behind you and bite
or is that camels?

You wouldn't be a camel
your bones aren't big enough.

I'd be a Labrador
slobber, slobber, pat me, pat me

at least I'd smile
not like you, you old sourpuss.

7

The sun still holds us
although your stiff

fingers are ice
and soon

the trees will send
shadows.

Let's get you home
your tea will be getting cold

but inside
a little voice is saying

what if she won't
what if she doesn't

what if we have to fight in public
explain to people?

It's fine.   Come on, Mum.   Yes
No.   We'll be right.   Thank you.

At the moment though
her feet are coming along

in the same direction
as mine.

Home comforts

Would you like some soup?

You know I don't like onions.
I didn't know that.
You've always had onions in soup.

I've never liked them.
Well there is onion in the soup,
just a little.

I've never liked onions.
Would you rather have an egg?

Oh no. I've had enough egg.
Is there anything you fancy?

Food doesn't agree with me.
A cup of tea?

I need to eat something, dear.

Hectoring

Can you sit down long enough to eat?
Please, will you just sit.

There, in my voice
I can hear it.
Hectoring!

Minding tone is
a relentless challenge.

Patience is worse
explaining patiently
could make me a saint

but in truth it would not be nice
using that ever patient tone.

Resentment

It's people I can't stand

asking things.

Left work now?
Got any plans?
How's things?
What you up to these days?
Been busy?

You mean now?

I'm planning onions.
It mightn't be
what I thought my future
would be
but here I am
with the shopping list
planning onions

which I hear tell
she doesn't even like.

What do you do?

Besides cooking soup, stew, casserole, porridge,
omelette, potatoes, pouring tea,
I sharpen knives,
mop the floor, change the sheets, wash dishes,
make doctor's appointment,
eye, skin, hearing appointment,
scrub the loo, stare at

the carcinogenic growths stuck on the inside of the oven walls
which I can't do anything about
without putting my head in the oven

iron pillowslips, light the fire, order wood, hang out the washing,
clean the shower, sweep veranda,
cut toenails,
do up her shoes,
clean her shoes,
find her shoes,
go shopping, put things away,
read advice from the Alzheimer's Care website
keep your loved ones busy it says

What do I do?
I stand in the garden shed sniffing petrol with my head in a cardboard box
scream very loudly without opening my mouth and
remember I should clean the car because it used to be Mum's
who would never have gone round in a rust bucket
but I crashed the back and the paint is peeling and it is going rusty

so why have I not rung the man at the garage?

I don't know, tell me
what do you do?

Searching for positivity

Things I like about my mother.

Two arms, two legs in working order
heart beats
stomach rumbles
in working order.

Eyes, ears, head, thoughts
I don't know
I just don't know.

I teeter.

My eyes are bigger now
and like a rabbit
my ears turn in all directions.

Home help day

In comes Sonia, Mum will be bathed
and I will go to the rescue home

where the dogs will be waiting
Fifi sitting in her corner looking nervous.

Do you mean me? she will say when I call her.
Her tail will move a little, brush the floor.

I wish someone would want her but
today she'll come to the beach with Raja and me

and Raja the Reckless will fling and corkscrew
leaving his ears in the air.

Fifi will run and return, run
and return, and on each return

her forget will nudge
at remember, forget will snuff

the fluffed-up foam
on the wave-strewn edge

as I watch the incremental draining
of the outgoing tide.

A matter of course

Monday

Outside Miss Bliss Hair and Beauty
I watch the woman
with two black greyhounds

she keeps them
muzzled

velvet elegant
handbags.

Tuesday

In the fug by the kitchen sink
there I am in the window
my body wearing bright purple
but no face
just a blurring of something sponged.

Wednesday

The trick is
to smooth the inside flap
of the pillowcases
using firm warm strokes
nuzzle the iron into their seams
flip and press the whole of the canker
before attacking shirt collars.

Mum helps me dance the sheets.

Thursday

In the supermarket, I see Belinda from work
the receptionist, a people-person
me, a lover of animals.

She has seen me, I need to speak
as if this other me inhabits words.
I pull on my enthusiastic face

how marvellous to see you what a shame I'm in
such a hurry meeting yes important friend-filled life
yes no she's good all good
and you
lovely

Friday

A quiver of fear, or is it shame
snatches at my heart when I meet people
and have nothing to say.

My tumbling walls make me lesser
diminish my world as I wing away
more and more to settle in the past, think

how once I met a man who sang
'Joshua Fought the Battle of Jericho'
while digging deep clods of thick black soil

how I saw a grinning frog splayed on the bedroom window
how I had a friend who pulled me
out of the river and agreed we would say nothing

how I had a mother who said you'd better look after this now
and put in my lap a round-bellied pup
and how we called him Pup

but now what to say
what to say now

Saturday

What's leaking
begging to be noticed
and unnoticed
pounding up the footpath
for a purpose
without a basket
in fact no handbag
carrying nothing
avoiding my mother

Sunday

I bargain with God
if I
speak nicely always
notice your good works
smile through the ironing
send money to the foundation
and not mind about the shoes in the bath
would you please take her to heaven with you?

Sunday evening is full of grace

Mrs Doyle from next door
is here, keeping an eye
sitting with her knitting
settling in to watch *I Want to Be*

I get in the car
drive to the beach,
where a soft grey man
stands on green lawn

his still arms, legs,
head, body, listening
his quiet self
considering the claret clouds

the silver water rippling
over silence, the no-colour sky
beyond the pink
holding a misted-over moon.

I'm another woman, not-me
hurrying to the shoreline
gazing up, out, over
from east to west

where the bruised sun is hidden
in hunched clouds
and the dark mountain rises.
This woman has no stillness

her fingers knit the air as she spins
determined to soak up her looking
before her domestic joyride
claims her again.

The man's reverie remains
and I return home
where Mrs Doyle explains
how to become a millionaire.

Slow drops of time

Something is raising its head
like cattle do

scrutinising
the empty paddock.

World without end amen
is the alarm.

Prison has time, has days
to mark off, on the wall.

Don't wish your life away
my mother once warned

when I wished only
that it was Friday after school.

Another year: another Monday

I clean the sink
with Ajax, heroic warrior.

With a nail brush
I threaten purple mould
growing in the corners, in the grooves
between the tiles on the wall and the sink.

I scrub at the rubbery grout
I need more Ajax
I need more.

The curtains
breathe in and out.

I lift my eyes, watch my mother
turn and turn again
her body doing
what her mind cannot
often
I wish
but
I have nothing to give.

Attempting a treaty

You're too cold, here put this on.
I try to wrap Mum in her cardigan

you're not nice, she says.
It's true, often I'm not
sorry, I say, I'm sorry
I don't like you, she says.

I don't want her
to say that
don't want her
to tell me that.

She pushes me
and a devil wildness rises
snarls behind my teeth
fills my eyes and ears

and I want to shake her
blame her completely.

I see her waiting
for me to hit her
frozen, fearful of me.

No, no, you're not going to
make me do that
and I walk out.

If it wasn't for the dogs' home
I don't know what I'd do.

A small offering

Once in the long ago
we kept dogs for constancy and comfort
and now from the dog's home
I bring in a small darkling pup

a rescue to rescue us
snuggled into my chest
spaniel ears and beagle blotches
about to enchant Mum

with dog musk and canine powers.
In the kitchen this dog prepares
to stem the current of our unease
by lapping water

scatters droplets in the way of baptism
and runs to meet Mum
ready for charmed leaping and licking
as an answer to our prayers

but Mum, primed
to ward off evil,
lifts her stick
and shouts protective words

Get that creature out!
It shouldn't be inside!
Don't let your mother
see that thing!

Pinpricks of anger engulf me
and my mother stops
bewildered
by her own voice.

It's not a dream

Midnight, almost held
in the balm of sleep
I hear the door click
voice, mumble, clatter
something in the kitchen.

She is putting the cups
into her walker
tipping oats in
tipping
orange juice in,
spilling it
on the floor
wiping it up
with a tea towel.
She's wet herself.

Again, again, again

I hold her walker
to pull her back to bed
I have to change her nightie
get her out of her wet stuff.
She's not talking

she makes noises in her throat
grabs my arms
her tongue
pushes her teeth out
she almost chokes

I force her onto the bed
hold her arms to the bed
hold her and sing.

Lullaby

Rock a bye baby
her arms are pinned down

in the tree top
I'm lying on top of her

when the wind blows
webs of spittle shimmer

the cradle will rock
I wish I could

give her drugs
when the bough breaks

the cradle will fall
the amount would be about

the same as for a Collie dog
down will come cradle

and baby and all
don't go there

eyes closed, our breath mingles
we lurch towards
unwanted exposure.

2 a.m.

People say she can't help it
I know she can't help it.

In the extreme heat
possums fall from trees

lie helpless on the footpath.
I can't help it either.

I have seen cows
flounder in deep mud.

Why is the *can't* help
always on her side?

We could both sleep
why can't we just sleep?

You thief!

*What are you doing
in my mother's body?*

When the time comes

just put me out of my misery

the words slip
from their night-time watch
into the morning

threaten
my wrists as I turn back
yesterday's cuffs.

If you put air in a syringe, can it kill you?

First rub the crook of the elbow
to find the vein.
Try the kindly pillow trick

using a hard downward pressure
or fling the wheelchair
under a passing train.

Whatever way
it will be used against me
in court, judge and jury

on the threshold of sympathy
towards people who knock off
those they care for

extenuating circumstances become mirrors.

Some lives mean more than others
and if they're going to die
before too long

who cares?

Redeemed by the mind's eye

I remember Kevvy's nose
his paws all hot hard leather.

With some dogs you have to let them
know you're in charge

but not Kevvy.
Eyes locked straight on mine

tail pounding the floor
he was boss. Get me up

in the mornings to the tumbling pleasure
of my fingers in his mouth, him

hauling me to join the day
explore each thrilling crevice

his different nature
ministering loveliness.

B flat in 3 minor parts

1.

I remember Lot's wife
was full of regret
immobilised by her past.

2.

I remember you looked so beautiful
after school
the way your coat hung down
in folds
and your lipstick.
You smelt like 4711.

3.

I remember
you gave us three meals a day.
That's not nothing.

Multiplicity

I stare at the computer
to reach out to the world
wanting to swallow it
see another me
that is not a mirror.

It offers
an intuitive interface

I can download an upgrade
and look, the government

will come on board
with a raft
a safety net.

Communion

I stopped at a church today
for polish and old wood comfort
wanting to believe, to see a point.

The priest walked over to me.
He was from Ghana.
I welcomed him
his shining loneliness.
We shared some sadness
but what could I do?

Mum's teeth

are in the bottom
of the pillowcase
I don't find them
until I hang out
the washing.

Good way to stop her biting.

Sometimes
when she's asleep in her chair

her stiff old legs
start scrabbling like a puppy
she huddles down
and whimpers
softly.

I hope she's chasing rabbits.

Check

She goes to lie down
but doesn't get up

she's a bit asleep
but thirsty all the time

wants to wee all the time
but I can talk to her

you'll be right it's ok
I stroke her

she knows I'm here
I think.

When help is needed

After hours
the phone goes through the night
to an Australia-wide service
with a long answering machine message

this call may be monitored for quality control
if you have a cold or flu-like symptoms
in an emergency ring 000
I know, I know…

A registered nurse! Thank the Lord.

She wants my Medicare number!
No, it's in the other room
sorry I wasn't thinking…
no I just want…

no you can't really…
she's not really conscious…
no I don't want…
I just yes but…

no I don't want to take her…
no you see…
her doctor is not…
I just want to talk

to a doctor
get a doctor over here…
no you can't speak
to the patient.
dear God

when Kevvy dog died
it was easy
pain, needle
all over.

Call the doctor service

Blessed relief
when I remember this service
where a doctor will come any time
so here I am, ringing them

with Health Card number
Medicare number
Gold card number
all here.

She says
Your suburb is out of the area
we can't come.

I say
We are fifteen minutes from the GPO
you must come!

She says
We have to draw the line somewhere.

I say
What line?
What line do you have to draw?
The bottom line is we need a doctor.
Is that too much to ask?
Has your mother ever died on you?
Have you watched her fight for breath
calmed her down
when she makes no sense
held her, cleaned her,
anything
to give you the right
to talk about lines?

All I want

is someone to listen.

No wonder I'd rather dogs.

Just imagine
a frenzy living in our backyard

glee written in her tail
her grin dripping over tongue and jowl

she cannot fit hours to a day
or seconds to a minute

smell and sound stretch endlessly
as she lies in readiness, alert to all good things

I imagine her name to be Rita
that she will chew a hole in my destiny.

How to measure time

Been busy?

It's a busy time a death

slow enough in coming
though later I'll say
thank goodness it was quick
and it is
this minute
less than a minute, less than a second
between life
and death

but slow

because of the hours
it takes the body
to come
to a complete stop.

Getting a grip

Perhaps her exiting
starts at seven o'clock in the morning
when she looks at me from a great distance.

Maybe it's the last time
I lift her on to the commode
and put her back to bed.

She needs to be higher up in the bed
but there is no connection
between her body parts.

The bed is too low

I keep thinking
if I get the right technique
I'll be able to lift her

the shrunken frame
of a disappearing woman
it can't be that hard

my whole mind resolute
as the bed bounces
and her body flops.

I can't get a grip.

I have forgotten
to order
disposable sheets to put under her.

I am no longer alone

The doctor is here
setting up an injection system.

The palliative care nurse is putting
a butterfly-clip
into her fallen flesh
giving her drugs
subterraneously.

The nurse tells me
how to draw up the injection
yes all right, I say

have you got that?
I think so
here I'll write it down

*this is how much
and the times
and you mark off
what you have given her.*

I mark off

what I have given her.

The small hours

Your nightie is wrinkled.
We must get those wrinkles out.

You're too cold.

Can you breathe better if I…?
Can I lift you up a bit?

The nurse said to wash her mouth out
with bicarb in the water.

I feel like
I am choking her with water

I keep trying to give her more.
Her chest patters

the soft puff
from her lips
stops.

Belonging

Her body
has given up the ghost

the Holy Ghost
God the Father, God the Son, God the Holy Ghost

and the ghost is the last bit
to melt away.

In the name of the Father
and the Son

or, the name of the Mother
and the Daughter.

In the life hereafter
I am what's left of her

my patterned cells signed by
the echo I tried to run from.

I open my mouth
out comes my mother.

A piece of business

I notice your teeth
think of the number of times
we lost them.

I don't know why I say we
I didn't lose them
I found them

smiling up from under your breast
or in the washing machine
grinning.

Now here they are
watching us
from the dressing table.

I know to put them
in your mouth
straight away

or they won't go
so I do
and catch myself smiling.

Biding

Death in these circumstances
is no unexpected thing

it is the small step
we have been waiting for.

It waits
while we wait

silent adjustment
poised in the present.

In the far-off sky
clouds are scudding.

There it is turbulent,
here, your not-being

is motionless
silent

leaving me
heartless

my limbs are connected
through habit

my feet walk
above the floor

my arms fold
into themselves.

At your funeral

I want to tell about the cold autumn
when we were mushrooming
and hidden birds pierced the thin silence of paddock mist
with rippling songs and whirrs berating
the dog's tracking through the bush;

how the cows stood away by the fence and I walked
on the other side of you because I didn't trust cows
but felt safe, leaning into you until we glimpsed
the polished tops and tender push of mushrooms
by the old pine trees;

how I raced like a colt to be the first of the pickers
but horror and dread, the cows came rasping and running,
all eyes and long horns galumphing towards me
now running scared and you calling to me, *stop!*
To the cows you called, *c'mon now, whoa now!*

You held up your arms and they stopped
but then you made me walk towards them
and I had to call, *c'mon now, whoa now!*
I wish everyone could have seen how the cows turned
sauntered back to the far fence and then heard you say

you're bigger than a cow.
Remember always. Bigger.

Today's lesson

On the veranda out the back
sitting in the last of the sun
I contemplate Dog who is old

and teaching me to contemplate slowly,
to brow-wrinkle over one eye.
Be satisfied with air, he instructs me

the glory of its breath
stirring night-time creatures
and he suggests I notice the smell

of Mrs Doyle's intention to cook lamb chops
reminding me of what we need to do now
in my familiar strangeness of empty rushing.

We listen as the house expands in soft slow clicks
and I reflect on how to teach Dog
that it is unnecessary to bark at possums.

Acknowledgements

When the Time Comes started life as a small piece of fictional writing reflecting the trickiness that confronted me after my mother turned eighty-nine and came to live with us. During that time, I sought advice and counselling from Carers Tasmania. There I met a diverse group of carers, all with very different stories. Inspired by their generosity and experiences, my writing grew and became a one-woman show called *Who Cares?* The production was assisted in its creation by Tasmania Performs and funding from Creative Hobart. *Who Cares?* was toured by Care2Serve Tasmania in 2020.

At the end of 2020, I decided to diverge again and turn the play into a collection of poems sequenced to form a narrative. The result is *When the Time Comes*.

When the Time Comes would not have been possible without the encouragement and support of family and friends. There have been many readers and generous storytellers in this process, and I thank everyone, named and unnamed.

Particular thanks go to Leigh Tesch, Sally Edith, Suzy Cooper and Ruth Hadlow for insisting I develop the original ideas, and always having faith in the outcome; Dr Gina Mercer for her immediate positivity, enthusiasm and practical guidance when the poems began to emerge; Chloe Meffre for her sensitive and fine editorial skills, clarity of thought and endless patience; Ruth Painter for sharing her love of language and proofreading the many final copies; and my partner Suzi Tyson for her unstinting partiality and goodwill.

Thank you to the daughters of Tasmanian artist Diana Mills (1923–2021) for their generosity in allowing her image to be used on the cover.

www.ingramcontent.com/pod-product-compliance
Lightning Source LLC
Chambersburg PA
CBHW071853031025
33557CB00052B/2629